"Have you done something wrong or failed? Don't worry, and feel no regrets. The life is very pleasant and also kind enough to offer some margin of errors to everyone, so there is no harm in consuming your quota of errors. Please, be happy and live every second of your life."

—A.K. SENGAR

READER'S DELIGHT

Life SIMPLIFIED

By
A.K. Sengar

Edited by
Anjani A. Gupta

READER'S DELIGHT
An Imprint of Ramesh Publishing House
NEW DELHI

ISBN 978-81-7812-728-6

Published by: Alok Kumar Gupta *for* Reader's Delight
(An Imprint of Ramesh Publishing House)

Admin. Office: 12-H, New Daryaganj Road, Opp. Traffic Kotwali,
New Delhi-110002 ✆ 23261567, 23275224 Telefax: 011-23275124

Showroom: • 4457, Nai Sarak, Delhi-6 ✆ 23918938
• 2604/16, Balaji Market, Nai Sarak, Delhi-6 ✆ 23253720

EMail: info@rameshpublishinghouse.com
Website: www.rameshpublishinghouse.com

INDEMNIFICATION CLAUSE

- *This book is being sold/distributed on the condition and understanding that the information given herein are merely for guidance and reference and must not be taken as authority, and neither the author nor the publishers individually or collectively, shall be responsible to indemnify the buyer/user/possessor of this book beyond the selling price of this book for any reason under any circumstances. If you do not agree to it, please do not buy/accept/use/ possess this book.*
- *Though every care has been taken in printing this book, errors or ommissions might have crept inadvertently. The publsihers shall be obliged if such error or ommission is brought to their notice.*
- *Subject to Delhi jurisdiction.*

© Publisher.

No part of this book may be reproduced or transmitted in any form or by any means, electronic or mechanical including photocopying, recording or by any transformation storage and retrieval system without prior permission from the Publisher.

Printed at: S.P. Printech, Delhi

Price: Rs 70/- only

A-63

Preface

The books like "Get, Set, Go" and "You can win" make me think whether to succeed and win is the sole aim of life. Why don't we emphasize on aspects of inner satisfaction and pleasure for ourselves? The emotional quotient is that a satisfied person is a successful person because he is not forcing himself to be a part of the mad race for reaching the 'top'. Further, a contented person is rarely critical of others and is able to derive pleasure even in little things he is able to accomplish. If you are not on the 'top' you are certainly not a looser. It all depends on what exactly you consider is being 'successful'. In my view, failures need more care so that the same situation, which caused them, does not arise again.

So far I have seen no such book which tells a person that he does not have to be above all to win in life. I am sure my book will offer the healing touch to those who are considered loosers by people who believe that being 'only' successful also means being happy.

The zest of the book is that it is more important to be satisfied than to be successful. I do not care how much fame and royalty is fetched by this book but it is my wish that it must reach the common people who may not opt only for success and win but want to lead a decent, peaceful and satisfied life.

— **AUTHOR**

❑❑❑

—A.K. SENGAR

About the Author

The author was born at Khandari in Agra in 1960 in a family dominated by teaching profession. He acquired his Master's Degree in Agriculture, and for the last 25 years he has been working as Manager in a Cooperative Dairy in Uttar Pradesh. His interactions with various people, specially those who are rural based, have inspired him to write this book for the masses.

Contents

Page No.

Life SIMPLIFIED

1

The Positivity

As a child, I was accustomed to hearing the preachings of elders that were meant to inspire me to be positive in life. But soon with the advance of age, I realised how much difficult it is to be always optimistic. No doubt, there are problems in our day-to-day life, but there are solutions too. So be very easy, solve those problems which you can, and leave the rest to be solved by destiny, which interacts with its own plans and ways. Everybody's mind must have a dustbin where worries without solutions are dumped and left for auto-degeneration.

Listen to the doctor within us who always prescribes the right remedy and the appropriate dose for our every problem.

According to ethics, we owe much towards our family, our society and nation but, prior to all, we first owe to 'ourself'. Unless we are at ease, we cannot put others at ease. There always exists a hidden doctor within every person, who can well diagnose the root causes of our biological and psychological illnesses. So, let us listen to the

If born then you are born to live and you just can't afford to die for any reason

doctor within us who always prescribes the right remedy and the appropriate dose for our every problem. There is no need to go for any kind of stress-management; have the habit of avoiding stresses because precaution is always better than cure. So again it is very simple: just try to elude the factors which cause strains and stresses, simply make the doctor within yourself dominant enough to command your thoughts and actions resulting in bud nipping of pessimism and generate room for positive thoughts. Please keep in mind that if you are born, then you are born to live and you just can't afford to die for 'any' reason.

2

Our Worries

The only thing, which segregates us from other species, is that only we humans have the capability to think, so we invite worries. The mere thought that we may fail in certain act, further aggravates this problem. A horse being trained for a race, does not have the worries of coming first; it simply has to run fast which involves only physical energy and its mind is never burdened with the result of race. Why can't we humans be like the above horse? Why the mere thought of being unsuccessful should disturb our peace? Make yourself accountable only for your efforts and do not hope for the guarantee of desired results.

Make yourself accountable only for your efforts and do not hope for the guarantee of desired results.

If we categorise our worries, only about 10 per cent of them are actual, 40 per cent of them are not related with us and the rest 50 per cent are virtual, because they will never occur but still we tend to speculate for everything. Take the load of only genuine worries that require attention and don't overburden yourself with unnecessary ones.

Take the load only of genuine worries

While boarding a train, if you are worried about proper fixing of rails, right signalling system and efficiency of drivers, you can never enjoy the journey. Here, again it is very easy, simply buy the proper ticket and prepare to enjoy your journey leaving the rest to the railway system. We being born as humans, should work systematically to enjoy the journey of life and leave the rest on the Almighty God who has his own procedures for providing auto-solutions of problems that are beyond our control.

There cannot be set guidelines for how to lead your life, the humanitarian weaknesses always play their part. Our religious book "The Geeta" preaches mankind only to worry for efforts and not to bother for result. But sometimes these teachings are hard to follow in normal life; how can you kill your cousine brother even if he is guilty; there is no soothing cream which can sole a father who has just lost his son. For a peaceful living, please don't be the creator of problems, instead be the mechanic of problems.

❑❑❑

3

Success And Failure

An Urdu poet has rightly said, "The success coming by invalid means to illegible persons has made me feel proud of my failures." Yes, sometimes our failures, too, need attention because in the long run they yield satisfying results. If something happens as per your wish, it is good, and if something goes against your aspirations then, at times, it may be good because destiny wants it to happen like that. Be sure that there may be hidden plans for your betterment in it. So why be afraid of failures, simply act in an optimistic way and accept the verdicts of God.

The failure in a certain section does not mean the end of everything.

Never try to over stress yourself mentally or physically when facing failure. First, try to run, if you cannot run then walk fast, if you can't do so then walk at ease, and if you can't even walk easily then learn to crawl; always keep yourself in motion because movement means life and no one wishes to be stagnant. What I am trying to say is — keep moving. Try different ways to be successful. So be at ease — work at the right time, in the right amount and in the right direction having a positive attitude.

The failure in a certain section does not mean the end of everything; instead it opens the doors of success in some other sector of life. A student who is poor academically may become a very good sportsman or businessman. So, fear of failure in getting good mark should not be allowed to dominate over his hidden efficiencies; it should not drive him away from taking bold decisions and actions. Be sure, an optimistic approach towards life will allow the flowers of destiny to bloom in your favour.

❑❑❑

4

Our Problems

Since we are born as human, the problems start arising right from our birth and end up only when our body reaches the burial ground. But the ill-effects of these problems during the course of life can be minimised if we segregate them according to merits and priorities. We have to keep in mind that we are simply a lone person and cannot combat all problems at an instant. We have humanitarian limitations, and it is impossible to tackle all problems at the same time. Some problems are so complex that their solution is beyond our control, so leave them alone and be sure that in the course of time they will find their own solutions.

The second type of problems are those which we have to solve ourselves. Now categorise them on the basis of urgency. First take the lower-merit problems which can be solved easily. By giving priority to solving the simpler problems first, there are more chances of success which will ultimately boost up our confidence and equip us with high morale and energy to face the complex problems. We often make this mistake of trying to take up complicated problems first and if somehow we fail, we loose our confidence and efficiency due to which we are unable to combat the simpler ones also.

The last kind of problems are of very minor nature and are the result of our psychological speculation. Such problems need virtually no attention because they automatically pass away with the passage of time.

Problems are an integral part of life and everyone living has to face them with varying quantum.

Never forget that problems are an integral part of life and everyone living has to face them with varying quantum. You can never get rid of them, as you solve one, another arises, and this process continues till you die. The problems act as a teacher too; they teach us lessons for the precaution and cures to minimise their reoccurrence.

Give priority to solving the simple problems first

So, again I would like to say that life is very simple, just try to be patient, do the best with your full efficiency and even then if you don't get the desired results, never feel guilty or regretful; just forget and march forward to get the best and try again to win in the next focussed destination.

❑❑❑

5

To Be Successful Or To Be Good

What does the society or a nation want its citizen to be? Successful ones or good ones? According to current trends, it is easier to be successful than to become a good citizen. By saying this, I don't conclude that all successful men are not good, but the tendency to apply all valid and invalid means to attain success drags people away from the path of goodness.

Now-a-days everyone wants success at any cost — the genuine values and goodness are in minority against appetite for success. This never-to-end appetite has ultimately caused all kinds of deformities in life. Now who is to be blamed for this? According to my view, we ourselves are responsible for this. Everyone praises a successful man but overlooks the ways he adopted to achieve it. I am not against wins and successes but the idea to attain success by all means, valid or invalid, makes me think that still a good man should be rated higher than a successful man.

Now, how do we define a good man? There may be several views about it but in simple terms, a good man is the one who is satisfied with himself and honest towards his family, society and nation. A successful man gains wealth and fame only for himself, but a genuine human brings laurels for the whole mankind. Since the path of success is easier than that of goodness, the demand for success always dominates the genuinity. In order to achieve success, one has to make many compromises and undergo various stresses. It is not mandatory that success would breed satisfaction. However, with goodness there is sure and certain guarantee of self satisfaction.

The tendency to apply all valid and invalid means to attain success drags people away from the path of goodness.

The success is termed as completion of anything which one intends to do, but it should only be welcomed if it is attained through ethical and genuine means. It may appear to the readers that I am trying to preach ideology but instead I want to convey that you should not loose the peace of mind even if the success is not attained.

You can succeed with invalid means but can never achieve goodness

A student, who is extraordinarily brilliant in studies, may migrate to a developed country for better perks and comfort. He may be rated as a successful man, but only for himself. According to my evaluation he fails to qualify as a good person because he has not contributed anything for the satisfaction of his ageing parents, society and nation. What I am saying is again very simple: try to lead a disciplined life with rationalized blending of success and goodness which is enough to bring the real satisfaction and contentment.

6

A Genuine Human

It is the prime duty on the part of every civilized society to have assessment factors for a good citizen and a genuine human. There is a continuous need for social audit so that pros and cons can be evaluated at regular intervals. The first step towards genuinity is the self-audit with positive attitude. Before contributing towards society or nation, one should contribute for himself.

The faith and confidence within oneself works like a catalyst in combating day-to-day challenges of life. Self-containment is must before preaching lessons to others and the genuinity should not be restricted merely to thoughts, it must also be revealed by actions.

The very first step towards genuinity is the self-audit with positive attitude.

Anything which gives you satisfaction but does no harm to others is genuine. All our actions should be guided by lessons from the past, should aim for the future, but the overall priority should be our present.

Be ready to help, but only upto the level till it does not kill your own interests and self-respect

As we belong to the civilized race, our heart always leads us towards ethics. But this ethical voice must be well-evaluated in the mind and then you should choose the action which suits your capabilities and renders ultimate satisfaction.

Apart from this, you should always beware of excessive genuinity which is often understood as weakness. If you are excessively polite at home, your family, relatives and neighbours will surely exploit you for their self-centered benefits. Similarly, if you are very humble and extra-ordinarily cooperative at your work place, your own colleagues will not hesitate in deriving undue advantage of your goodness. No doubt, you should always be ready to help, but only upto the level till it does not kill your own interests and self-respect.

It is, therefore, very important that along with responsibilities, the rights must also be known. Just listen to your heart but work according to your brain, this would surely lead you towards creativity as well as goodness. And the overall interpretation of your personality in the eyes of others would be that of a genuine human.

❑❑❑

7

The Right Dose Of Sincerity

People may have different experiences about the outcome of sincerity; sometimes it is a boon and sometimes a curse too. If you are excessively sincere about something and if it does not go according to your wishes, you tend to develop frustration and depression. In my view, only proper amount of sincerity at the right time and at the right place is recommendable. I noticed during my school days that the day I cleaned and oiled my bicycle, it surely got punctured, but on the day when I did not care to clean it, it was never out of order. Later on, I realized that cleaning the bicycle is not the guarantee of its fitness, instead the condition of tyres and tubes plus the road were more responsible for it.

Have a balanced attitude and simply don't try to be too sincere towards anything, and at the same time don't expect return benefits. I have seen people getting worried even when their puppy suffers from indigestion or their car has a minor dent. Now this is over-sincerity because indigestion and dent are very simple and common events. There are many medics and mechanics in the market who can well take care of them, so why unnecessarily put mental stress on yourself. Keep in mind that even if you loose your puppy and feel depressed for a while, it will not be the end of everything, and if you don't remove the minor dents, still, your car will be road-worthy.

> ***Proper amount of sincerity at the right time and at the right place is recommendable.***

If a parent is overcaring about his children, they will develop the habit of spoon-feeding. In one case, Mr. X. had the routine of awakening his son for school-time though the later had an alarm-clock too. If not awakened, the child would continue sleeping till noon. One day Mr. X. decided not to awake him and as a result, when the child reached the school late, he was scolded by his teacher. This fear of being scolded ultimately made the child cautious and he awoke by himself on time in future.

Sometimes over-sincerity makes people take you for granted. You then get very little time for yourself and gradually your own priorities get disturbed. Be sincere to help others too, but at the same time don't ignore your own interests. No doubt, some priority matters may need sincerity but not all, and if we try to face all at a time, there are chances of total failure.

It is, therefore, necessary that you must have self-respect for yourself and not allow anyone to misinterpret your over-sincerity. Simply act as per your ability with balanced amount of sincerity keeping in view that you owe a lot towards yourself than owing to others.

❑❑❑

8

Everyone Is Different

By virtue of nature and destiny, no two person are born alike. They may be similar in few aspects but vary on many other features. Physically they may be same but their thoughts and concepts about life are mostly different. Each person has his own perceptions of life and tries to negotiate things in his own ways guided by his inner abilities and previous interactive experiences. So, you should never try to impose your own ideas on others and whosoever tries it repeatedly invites problems for himself. The situation is so grave that even your own children and family may not heed to your thoughts and guidance, resulting in unnecessary

Each person has his own perceptions of life and tries to negotiate things in his own ways.

mental stress at both ends. Simply, let everyone lead his life in his own way.

Everyone chooses what he wants to be and leads life accordingly

The advice should be given only when it is sought, and with the caution that if it fails to work, the blame should not rest on your shoulders. Everyone lives and works in different conditions and his thoughts and actions are shaped according to his own environment. If someone misses a train, there are three options for him: wait for next train, cancel the journey, or opt for some other means of transport. Here you cannot force your advice on him because his decision will depend on his planned time schedule and urgency of work.

Everyone has a hidden teacher within him. So, let this teacher teach you first and avoid the human tendency to rule rather than to be ruled. If during the leisure time, a playing child is asked to study, he may momentarily follow you, but in reality his studies during that time will be of no use because of lack of concentration. In the same way, if someone has interest in medicine, and is forced to go for engineering, chances are that he can never become a good engineer. Therefore, let everyone lead his own life, you may only guide the others at certain junctures, but never feel annoyed if your guidance and advice is not followed exactly. A religious teacher preaches many things, but it is not guaranteed that all his disciples will follow exactly what he has preached.

It must be kept in mind that the Almighty God has predecided plans for everyone and no power on earth can change it. Your interceptions and efforts are of no use. The fate will, in due course, take you to the right place at the right time as per the wishes of destiny.

So, again it is very simple: just realise that we are small creations of God, we have humanitarian limitations and cannot run the world as per our wishes. Everyone chooses what he wants to be and leads life accordingly. No two people in the same profession can be found leading a similar life or having same thoughts. So, just let everyone be what he or she is.

9

Be Proud Of Yourself

You cannot possibly bring pride to your family, society and nation unless you are proud of yourself. Self-appreciation generates enormous self-confidence which serves as a tonic when we face depression. The sole idea that you are the best creature on this earth is strong enough to make you feel proud of yourself. Here, the word proud should not be mistaken with rudeness because rudeness implies negativity whereas pride has blending of self-respect.

When we admire others, there is surely a parallel hidden feeling of regret for ourselves, but when we admire ourselves, we generate within us positive energy and ideas for the betterment of our future. When we repair a minor fuse wire at our home, we may not save much money but it surely gives us satisfaction and self-respect. Similarly, the fruits of all positive actions taken by us are enough for our self appeasement, and actions leading towards negativity should be taken as the lesson for future actions.

When we admire others, there is surely a parallel hidden feeling of regret for ourselves, but when we admire ourselves, we generate within us positive energy and ideas for the betterment of our future.

We work very hard and apply all valid and invalid means to win and attain success which ultimately brings us satisfaction. Nonetheless, if we do not win or succeed, the mere idea that we applied only genuine means, will help us to overcome the sorrow of failure. Consider this: Mr. 'A' has secured 90 per cent marks in certain exam but still he curses himself because a few students have scored more than him. Instead, Mr. 'B' has got only 70 per cent marks in the same exam, but he is still very pleased with himself because last time he got 65 per cent marks.

Similarly, in our day-to-day life we come across many small things happening in our favour; so

"I have done the best"

why can't we derive satisfaction from them? Let us activate the sieve within ourselves which should retain all positives of the day and allow unfavourables to filter away as residues. While going to bed after a hectic day, rememorize the positives retained — this will bring you self-satisfaction and a sound sleep. Putting it simply, be proud of yourself for all positives you have achieved and that you are ready for another day without any negativity.

❑❑❑

10

You Are The Best

As the self-appreciation is the best remedy for depression, the habit of self-praise works as a great morale-booster. The ultimate theory that you live only once, you did not exist before, and will not exist in future should prompt us for the better utilization of our life. Whatever we do and earn, should be for the sole aim of our satisfaction keeping aside the quantum of successes and wins. If the cost of success and win is higher than our capacity, let us concentrate on smaller things within our reach and derive satisfaction from them.

The feeling that your are the best, is the pre-requisite for all your positive creations.

The feeling that you are the best, is the pre-requisite for all your positive creations. The humans are superior to other species because they have advanced brain functions with ability to memorise and think. Animals and insects too have brain but their actions are merely based on instincts and inherited habits. The only thing, which demarcates us from other species, is our varied perceptions of life based on previous memories and individual ideology.

A dog barks at every intruder, whether a friend or foe, because it is his habit, but such kind of action is not expected from us. Being superior, we have the ability to perceive, evaluate and act as per the merit and need of the situation. The head of the family enjoys some privileges, but he has to bear the load of responsibilities too. Similarly, it may sound cozy that we are the superior race, but it brings us a crown of thorns also. So, we just cannot escape by behaving randomly, the thought that we are humans itself is catalytic but the idea that 'I am the best' works as a great morale-booster.

All appreciated persons in the world have brain, limbs and organs similar to you and this physical similarity is enough to encourage you to work for betterment. The only thing, which made them great, was the higher percentage of success than yours. So, never give up trying to the best of your efforts.

Your positive attitude and genuine efforts are enough to give you the satisfactory feeling that you are the best. And even if you don't prove to be the best, at least have the psychological feeling of being the best. Now, please stop cursing yourself; instead, just praise your efforts and thank God that at least you have one thing best in you, *i.e.*, you are a capable human.

Your positive attitude and genuine efforts are enough to give you the satisfactory feeling that you are the best.

□□□

11

Never Exhibit Your Weakness

The strengths and weaknesses are an integral part of human character. As the darkness is must to realise the importance of light, the strengths of ones character cannot be unearthed unless there are behavioural weaknesses. It is the natural tendency of every person to exploit the weakness of others, therefore be cautious; never reveal your loose ends to others.

Your weaknesses are your private property, so instead of feeling regrets, accept them pleasantly without making complaints.

There are two types of weaknesses. The first type are short-lived and are developed as a response to certain unfavourable factors. These need no special attention because they automatically vanish as the causing factors pass away. For example if a child fails in an exam, he may develop the shyness of facing his promoted classmates. This weakness will end naturally when he passes the exam next time.

The second kind of shortcomings are of serious nature, which may be inherited or arise during our life span. Now, take it for granted that however hard you try and toil, these permanent natured weaknesses will never end. So, you need not regret about these and instead, learn to live with them. Your loose ends will harm you only when they are revealed to others. A friend of mine cannot tolerate waste papers lying on floor. Even in office he used to pick up the waste papers thrown by his co-workers. The more he tried to keep the floor clean, the more papers were deliberately thrown by others. Had his colleagues not known this weakness, he would have saved himself from humiliation.

The exploiting conditions are even faced at home level too. Your own near and dear ones may also loose no chance of taking undue advantage of your weaknesses. Sometimes, you may be at the receiving end but you never realise it because it has become a part of your character. When it is certain that you cannot get rid of a particular weakness; don't worry; try to live up with it and draw enjoyment from it. Just have the thought that you are simply a human and all the factors are not under your control; your weaknesses are your private property, so instead of feeling regrets, accept them pleasantly without making complaints.

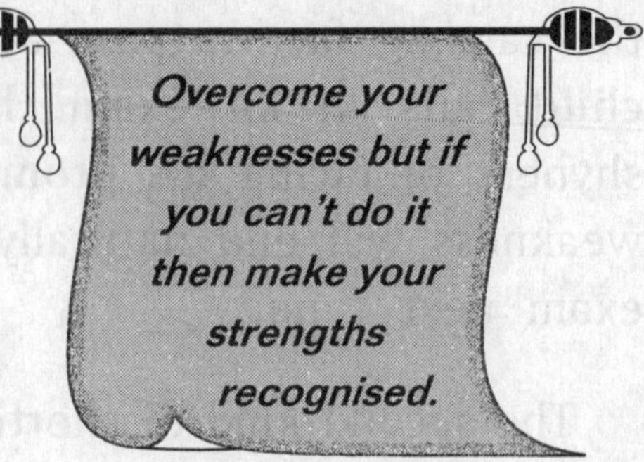

There is no sieve through which we can retain all the strengths and get rid of weaknesses. Our strengths and weaknesses both, ultimately, continue to run altogether throughout our life. So, please learn to accept yourself in totality; love your strengths but at the same time don't hate your weaknesses. Try your best to overcome your weaknesses but if you can't do it, then make your strengths recognised so that others don't get a chance to get anywhere near your weaknesses.

❑❑❑

12

Know Your Limitations

As no two persons in the world are alike, their capacity to grasp and the capability to perform under different environment is also different. The varying capacity and capability to perform depends upon gender and physical and mental health, but the conditions under which we live also play a vital role.

It is important that we should not have any illusions about ourselves. Before trying to assess others, we must have an accurate assessment of 'ourself'. Set your goals keeping your efficiencies in mind. If you realise that your capacities and capabilities are not enough to achieve a certain aim, then don't try for it. If you still go for it, then there are more chances of failure and your efforts will go waste, which will ultimately bring frustration and depression. So, first assess yourself and then act according to your capabilities.

It is always good to have aspirations but only till they match the worth of your abilities and do not disturb the peace of your mind. You must learn to accept happily what you have attained and try to draw satisfaction out of it. Mr. 'A' had become the manager in his bank by applying all valid and invalid means but still he was not happy because he regreted for not being able to become the general manager. On the contrary Mr. 'B', who was a mediocre student and was selected for a clerical job found himself more satisfied because he knew that his abilities only permitted him to become a clerk. If, still, he had kept on trying for higher post, he would have only invited various stresses for himself.

The persons, who are unable to estimate themselves, tend to go after everything and in the end achieve nothing.

The persons, who are unable to estimate themselves, tend to go after everything and in the end achieve nothing. In a football team, the capabilities of goalkeeper and forward players are different; a good forward cannot be a good goal-keeper and a good goal-keeper cannot be a fine forward player. There are certain limitations of both and their position in the team is decided as per their efficiency. This simply means that a goal-keeper should feel satisfied and enjoy his own role; at the same time he should not aspire to become a forward player. The same theory holds for the forward player too.

First access yourself and then act as per your capabilities

According to my view, the destiny is kind enough to give us what we deserves according to our abilities. Though it is not good to be over ambitious nevertheless, the offered chances also should not be lost. If something is accessible without taking stresses, you must opt for it, but if you feel that it is beyond your reach, don't think of trying for it first. It is quite true that everyone cannot achieve everything; if we had this exceptionally unique feature, we would have become God. We are humans and let us remain and behave like humans.

You must be true to yourself by having a justified evaluation of your capacities and capabilities and draw satisfaction and happiness from whatever you have attained with ease as well as with your maximum efforts.

❑❑❑

13

Don't Live In Fool's Paradise

Many people try to run away from the hard realities of life and live with many kinds of illusions. This trend cannot continue for long because very soon day-to-day interactions teach them lessons which are must for practical life. You cannot brush aside problems, the matters whose solution exists should be tackled immediately on merit and problems whose remedy is beyond your control should be deferred. This postponement of complex situations may lead to auto-solution or give you chance to recoup your vigour to face them boldly. So, please don't adopt an escapist attitude and don't make your own unpractical paradise to fool yourself. Have courage to face the problems, put down your best efforts and leave the rest on the Almighty God.

We must realise that our duties vary according to the stages of life. As a child we don't face many problems because our parents take care of us; as a student, as we should, we pay prime attention to our studies; and as an adult we have to be sincere about our family plus our profession. We should adopt those ways which bring ease to our life but this does not imply that we should be careless. As a human, everyone has the right to choose his own ways of self-satisfaction. At the same time, any appeasement, which takes you away from realities, leads to the creation of foolish illusions. If you are physically weak and want to become a wrestler, it is certainly a harmful thought. On the other hand, you should develop other interests which match your physical and mental abilities.

You cannot wait for miracles to happen because they do not happen with everyone, everytime and there exists nothing like a magic stick.

The false assessment of situations when grown in large magnitude, create hinderances in normal functioning of life. Though I opt for simplicity and easiness in life, I don't mean that you should be negligent. Be sure, dreams cannot face the storms of reality, so exercise caution before dreaming becomes a chronic problem. You cannot wait for miracles to happen because they do not happen with everyone, everytime and there exists nothing like a magic stick or the Aladdin's lamp. Don't be foolish; to catch a fish you have to be near water. You just can't think of sitting for away from water because you are scared of it and dream of a mouth-watering fish preparation for dinner.

Don't be foolish; to catch a fish you have to be near water

Our illusions may sometimes give temporary relief from stress but can never give a permanent solution. We must hear the voice of our inner being and our actions should not be based on false assumptions but should be guided by actual facts. So, do not always be dreamer; wake up and find the right path to lead a satisfying life.

❑❑❑

14

Life Classified

The journey from maternity ward to grave yard can be categorised into various stages. Each stage of life has its effect on the next. If this linkage gets coordinated well, you feel satisfied and pleased. The very first event — the birth plays an important role in deciding our fortune. One cannot decide when and where he or she will be born because it is decided only by destiny. Your birth was the result of coincidental physical act of your parents, but they too cannot dictate your fortune.

Each stage of life has its effect on the next. If this linkage gets coordinated well, you feel satisfied and pleased.

An infant or a child cannot retain memories; his brain is not mature enough to evaluate; and his activities depend totally on the way he is cared for by his parents. There are no prescribed duties for a child, but the parents have to play their role like a gardener. If the saplings are nursed well, the upcoming plants will surely bear beautiful flowers and sweet fruits. Similarly, the parental care and home environment plays the most important role in the making of a justified human. Therefore, we cannot expect much from a child; he simply has to eat, play and sleep with a little pinch of instructed basic learning and studies.

The childhood is followed by adolescence, and this is the stage from where the actual grooming starts. It is just like soldiers getting ready for a war. At this level the child's brain starts percepting and reacting to the surrounding environment. This is the time when the real strengthening takes place. However, still at this stage the child cannot exist independently. His proper upbringing needs continuous parental guidance and inspiration. He gradually learns by trial and error method and

If the saplings are nursed well, the upcoming plants will surely bear beautiful flowers and sweet fruits.

starts visualizing the world from his own angle. With adolescence come ambitions. So, at this level the child should be taught and guided to learn to access himself and develop only those aspirations which suit his abilities. If at this stage one tends to become over ambitious, be sure, he is laying a false foundation which will have negative effect on his future life.

Please enjoy your journey from birth till final exit

In most advanced countries, the adolescents are mostly left independent to live their own life which ultimately results in formation of non-cohesive societies where members lack sentiments for each other. In order to generate a sensitive society, the parental rider is must so that the adolescent learns social etiquettes. Adolescence is the most crucial stage of life where, apart from studies etc., he should start feeling the sense of responsibilities too. But if simply loaded with huge quantum of duties at this tender stage, he may feel confused and perturbed. It is, therefore, required on the part of parents to behave like a friend, philosopher and guide at this crucial juncture of their child's life.

The adolescence is followed by adulthood which simply means the final genesis of a physically and mentally matured person. An adult is the backbone of society and the foundation brick of a strong nation. Therefore, at this age, he has to be most sincere and rationalized in his behaviour. His actions have direct impact on the overall well being of his family and society. By this stage, he has completed studies and starts earning; he is loaded with responsibilities, official and social. There is every fear that the tendency to win and succeed may become so intense that it may result in an over ambitious personality. As everyone has an inner urge to rule, one wants to rule at home and outside too. He may succeed to some extent at home but it should never be expected that one can rule over every one and everytime. He should have no confusion at this stage; being the master of his house he may have the right to rule but should never try to dictate. The situation becomes more grave when plenty of ambitions get blended in and when not fulfilled, result in many kinds of complexities and frustrations.

An adult is the backbone of society and the foundation brick of a strong nation.

The prime expectations from a genuine adult are that he should have clear-cut priorities based on his available resources. Though these may vary from person to person, there always exists an ideal set of three priorities. The very first priority lies towards yourself. If you are able to keep yourself healthy and mentally balanced, then only can you perform according to the expectations. A physically weak or ill person is a liability for himself and his family. If he is mentally sick too, he becomes a burden on the whole society. So, first of all one should learn to keep oneself fit and adopt ways which keep one at ease. The simple theory is that you cannot give something unless you have it yourself. During a journey, you can lift others' luggage only if first you are able to lift your own. Similarly, you cannot lend money to others unless you have it yourself. Be rest assured that you cannot satisfy others until you are satisfied with yourself. So please, first consider satisfying yourself and then try to appease others.

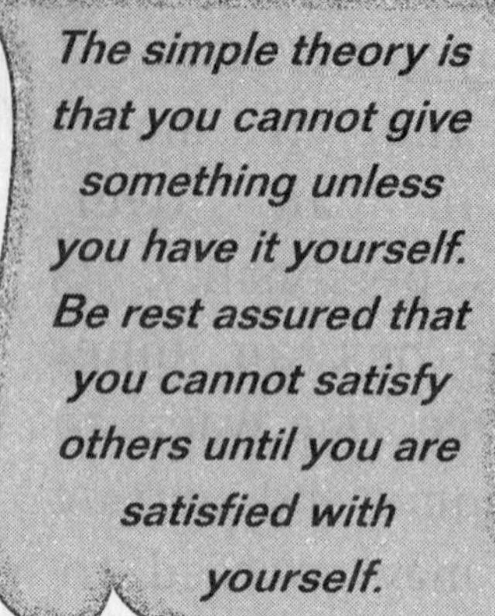

Your duties and responsibilities towards your family stand second in the priority list. You should well nurse and love your children, spouse, parents and near and dear ones because whatever you are doing or earning, it is for the welfare of your family. The ugly lure to succeed and win, sometimes makes us so self-centred that we neglect our family. Since every adult is the guardian of his family, the lack of proper guidance and care results in the birth of a scattered family and an unmeaningful society. Within a family, some common matters have easier solutions but some need to be dealt with heavier hands. So, don't let anyone take you for granted, deal with them on merit and always maintain your cool. Your family needs you, be ideal for them and adopt the theory of live and let live.

The third priority should always be your source of earning, whether a job, business or any other kind of profession. One should always be justified towards one's profession because it brings earnings which are much needed to run the family and provide them respectable social identity. Work as hard as you can but never overstress yourself physically and mentally. Here, you should be wise enough to safeguard your own interests first so that no one can take undue advantage of your genuinity. Be more practical and have lesser room for emotions. After this third priority, all other priorities depend on one's individual will and nature which she or he is free to decide according to personal living, working environment and situations.

There is no set age limit when one can be identified as an adult. The main indicator commonly accepted is the beginning of decline in physical abilities. The other factors may be that responsibilities have already reached their peak and no new responsibilities are due to come up for his attention, *i.e.*, he has successfully completed all his responsibilities or is on the verge of completing them. He has faced all experiences of life — sweet or bitter — and learned lessons from them. Though, by the end of adulthood, the physical efficiencies begin to recede but the mental abilities are at maximum. Generally these symptoms are seen around 50 years of age. At this stage, a man's condition is 'just like that of any athlete who has just now completed his race and is getting ready to pack up his kit'.

A few people may try to prolong their adulthood by feeling and showing that they are still young from within but it is mandatory that at some juncture this period is bound to end and reflect on their personality likewise. The people in their fifties need to be more cautious and passified in their behaviour. It now becomes obligatory that the person starts containing himself. Also it is ethical that by this stage he should stop being adventurous. He should try to have little rest, evaluate his past performances and then try to complete his remaining personal and social obligations with an easy and dignified pace.

The end of adulthood does not mean concealment of all the pleasantries of life. It only conveys that now one should limit his aspirations and feel satisfied with his achievements. Even if something has not gone according to one's wishes, one should accept it as the gift of God, try to retain the positives and forget the unfortunate moments. Now, as one enters into sixties, one is expected to be free from most of one's responsibilities and the phase of withdrawl begins. By this time he would have retired from active life. He should try to utilize his leisure time in social or other kind of activities which give him pleasure. Let the memories fade away because not remembering everything at old age keeps one at ease.

There is no set code of conduct for old age.

This is the stage of life when there is no time for any regret and complaint. Every person must feel contended that he has performed to the best of his ability and resources, and thank God for whatever he has been offered. There is no set code of conduct for old age; now one is totally free and independent to do what gives one joy and satisfaction. At the same time, one should prepare oneself mentally for 'packing up' and though it is not in one's hands, opt not for a belated staggering departure but prefer a fine satisfying final exit.

15

Live Only For Today

The existing fact, that past has gone and future is not known, forces the present to dominate over the two. A person should have the courage to evaluate his past religiously and sieve out odds to retain positives only. It is certain that you may have done many wrongs, some knowingly and some involuntarily. The later need not be cared about because it comes within the preview of humanitarian limitations but mistakes committed voluntarily should teach us lessons and they should not be repeated. Just forget your past and forgive yourself. You should not feel worried for the future because though you may have laid solid foundations and prepared yourself for it, the final decision lies with destiny. Please be assured that the Almighty God always has plan A, B or C for you, thus never feel perturbed. If one plan fails, some other will come for your rescue and even if you do not succeed, your justified efforts should give you the feeling of satisfaction.

Out of the three time tenses above, the present always has an upper hand because it is within your reach. It is the ultimate truth that you begin to move closer to death right from the very moment you are born. Every second of time passing by is shortening your life and nearing you towards death. So, one must live every second of his life. Since life is the most precious gift of God, please don't waste it, learn to live it. Though I do realise that practically it is very difficult to forget the past because memories cannot be erased easily; but the mental load of unfavourable experiences can be minimized with positive thoughts. Please note that you are simply one creature who is bound to

You begin to move closer to death right from the very moment you are born. Every second of time passing by is shortening your life and nearing you towards death. So, one must live every second of his life.

have weaknesses and sky is not going to fall if anything goes wrong.

Don't loose your present for the uncertain future

There are so many stressing factors which are always ready to disturb us and lead to wrong ways. The thought, that we all have humanitarian weaknesses and things always do not happen as per our wish, will surely help in reducing the ill-effects of past memories. We must learn to accept the things in totality, it is next to impossible to retain only the good ones and neglect the bad ones. Our natural limitations always allow room for forgiveness and one must learn to forget and forgive himself. So, have faith in yourself and realise that you are not blessed with extra-special powers to control everything. Therefore, you must finally care for your present only. Do not loose your present for the uncertain future.

The lessons from past and aspirations for future are the guiding force for creating a pleasant present.

You cannot, or rather should not, loose your present for the sake of past too. The present is with you and you have every chance to mould things for your ease. The lessons from past and aspirations for future are the guiding force for creating a pleasant present. There are thousands of theories advocating incarnation and reincarnation but the ground truth is that you live only once. Therefore, you cannot afford to let your present go waste. You have a healthy and an advanced brain to evaluate well, and supportive limbs. So, do not hesitate in applying all possible efforts to beautify your present, and luckily if you have your part of luck too, you will achieve the goals. Simply, keep your efforts uptodate and do not care for the results; feel no panic if the outcome is not favourable, just be patient and think of alternative paths.

There is always a certain quantum of luck in the basket of destiny which is not poured all at a time but it is released sustainably at suitable instances. So you can never know when your part of good luck is going to improve your life. What you can do, is only to put down your capable efforts and wait for the outcome. Be brave to accept whatever you have been offered and do not waste your present in unnecessary evaluations. Be known, that there exists no blue book of rules as to how you can make your present enjoyable. Simply, have positive attitude and try to extract joy from every moment, relieve yourself from pressure of the past which has already by gone, and do not care much for the future because things will happen only as per the plan of destiny. Many times our over sincerity and

Laugh at your past, smile at your present and get ready to welcome a bright future.

thorough gentleness causes hurdles in allowing us to sail joyfully because the pressure of perfectionism always causes many kinds of stresses. It is, therefore, advisable not to always act emotionally. A proper blending of practicality is must to safeguard your interests.

Having a satisfying present automatically opens the doors for the future suiting your aspirations. No one can steal your portion of luck and, at the same time, no one can add to it. Therefore, you are bound to receive your share of fortune, which varies from person to person. There must be many things that we think are beyond the reach of our resources, but still we tend to aspire for them. Such aspiration may have already contaminated your past, still effecting your present and, as a result, are bound to destroy your future too. It is, therefore, wiser not to try for such ambitions and invite frustration to create a self-generated hell. Since only efforts are under your control and not the destiny, have mercy on yourself, laugh at your past, smile at your present and get ready to welcome a bright future.

❑❑❑

16

Theory Of Benefits

A famous urdu poet has rightly said, "What is the benefit of benefits." This theory professes that one should not only look for benefits but should also seek satisfaction. The attainment of benefits may lead to success and wins, but it is not compulsory that it will provide satisfaction too. Now-a-days, it is the period of cut-throat competition, therefore, the hunt for benefits is very strong. When the resources are limited and aspirants are more, it leads to the birth of unethical practices resulting in a selfish society. The world will become a real heaven if people do not ask only for self-benefits

> ***The attainment of benefits may lead to success and wins but it is not compulsory that it will provide satisfaction too.***

but follow the principle of live and let live. If one asks for larger dose of benefits, be sure he is becoming selfish and snatching away the rights of others.

Do not look only for benefits but also seek satisfaction

The real benefit of benefits lies when you put yourself at ease and appease others too. Upon seeing a banana skin lying on the road, a selfish man may curse the culprit and move away allowing some one else to fall, but a genuine person will simply throw it aside before proceeding further. A person who is always after benefits may become a successful professional but can never be a genuine person. The flight for benefits should never be so strong that it leads you away from your other priorities. It is the ultimate fact that we all will die because death is inevitable; so, one should realise this truth and give weightage to happiness over benefits. We have been born empty-handed and will finally exit empty-handed, all benefits, wins and successes are bound to be left behind. So, why to toil unnecessarily and victimise ourselves of over ambitiousness. Let us accept the things in the way as they come and feel satisfied that destiny is giving us what we deserve.

The real benefit of benefits lies when you put yourself at ease and appease others too.

The time does not remain the same always, there are ups and downs, so we must be ready to accept both as the offerings of the Almighty. The advantages derived from benefits can never compete with satisfaction because such advantages are short-lived. You may bypass many red signals to get the benefit of reaching earlier, but such benefits will be of no use if you get legally penalized at some juncture. So, kindly do not feel the hunger for benefits only, feel satisfied with your limited assets and be thankful to God for his offerings — whether sweet or bitter.

17

Be Your Own Navigator

If you are worried, perturbed and confused, then please enter your navigational cockpit — the brain. Here, you will find every instrument to monitor your miseries. Our soul always keeps on demanding explanations from ourselves for what we do but, at the same time, also torches the right path to be taken. So, try to hear yourself and heed to its directions. You have every right to be proud of your contributions and achievements, but don't be biased in accepting your failures. The success and failure are the two faces of the same

Our soul always keeps on demanding explanations from ourselves for what we do but, at the same time, also torches the right path to be taken.

coin called life and since these are unseparable, you have to accept both with open mind.

There always exists an advocate, a mechanic and a doctor within everyone's core and plays prime role in guiding his life. If, while driving a car, we overstep the speed without changing gear, the vehicle itself starts giving indications by heavy engine sound for changing the gear, and if we overlook it, we are probably heading for an accident. Similarly, if some unjustified idea comes in our mind, our soul never fails to give remedial signals, and if we don't heed to it, surely we are asking for trouble. The immunity power within everyone plays its preventive role till our thoughts and actions are within permissible limits. Once we cross the limits, we are bound to go on a wrong path. A person consuming alcohol within limits may be tolerated, but once he exceeds the intake, he gets branded as an alcoholic and invites all kinds of mental, physical and social distresses for himself. Therefore, it is mandatory to keep all the navigating instruments

Your self - navigations should also match with the need of time.

within your control so that you can mould everything around you according to your priorities and social ethics.

You are your best navigator

One often feels frustrated when one realizes that inspite of all justified efforts, the desired results are not obtained while some achieve their goals without much toil. In such situations, you can only pacify yourself with the thought that your correct navigation and efforts failed simply because you did not have enough luck in your favour while the others enjoyed the support of destiny. This doesn't mean that a few failures should distract you from adopting right options; just be optimistic and wait calmly for your share of destiny to favour you.

Your self-navigations should also match with the need of time, never be too fast or too slow — try to have a mediocre approach. Since the mediocres are always in majority, we can enjoy more and keep ourselves free from all kinds of stresses, but when we try to pose ourselves as "very special" we fall in minority which may render uneasiness to us. So, kindly love yourself, listen to your inner advocate, let the mechanic within you to rectify your faults and heed to the prescriptions of the doctor in your core to generate accurate self-navigational skills needed for a peaceful and pleasant life.

Love yourself, listen to your inner advocate, let the mechanic within you to rectify your faults and heed to the prescriptions of doctor in your core.

❑❑❑

18

Learn To Say 'No'

Many friends of mine launch themselves in distress because they simply cannot say 'No'. It is a behavioural weakness which carries a lot of miseries with it. There is always a chance that this habit of any person can be well exploited by others; they may just transfer all their load of responsibilities and problems onto his shoulders without caring for his ease. The poor fellow simply accepts these distresses because he does not have the habit of saying 'No' to anyone. Such people are taken for granted by their near and dear ones, and in return may get some appreciation. These people must realise that they

Not being able to say 'No' is a behavioural weakness which carries a lot of miseries with it.

are paying a very high cost for this suicidal habit because voluntarily they are killing their own interests somewhere or the other.

Beware of exploitation, please say, "No"

As we are living in the sensitive society, it is always good to be helpful but only till it does not disturb your own comfort. There are surely some moments when you have to make adjustments and compromises with others but please take care of your ease first. While accepting to help others, you must weigh all the possible outcomes; if you think that it is not putting you under stress, then go for it but if you feel that it may put you under stress, be brave to say 'No'. For a sensible person there is no harm in supporting others even if he has to sacrifice a little of his comfort, but he too must always be aware that it should not become a regular habit. Differences are always there between selfish people and sensible ones. A selfish person, first of all, will not be easily ready to help others and even if he agrees he will prefer to fulfil his own interest first. At the same time, a sensible person will take care of others along with his own ease.

Teach yourself to say 'No' or else you will be like Mr. 'X' and Mr. 'Y'. Mr. 'X' has to buy many pens during the month because he cannot say 'No' to anyone who asks for it, and the receiver is also not sincere enough to return it. The car of Mr. 'Y' is mostly out of order because habitwise he never denies in lending it even to friends and relatives who are careless and never take the worry to drive it carefully. Here, Mr. 'X' or Mr. 'Y' have got the social taboo of being very helpful but nobody takes care to estimate or understand the agony they have to face.

Note that in a blood donation camp you are allowed to donate only a limited quantity of blood so that there is no ill-effect on your health. The same ideology should be applied when taking decision to help or rescue others. First evaluate the pros and cons of your action and if the situation permits, feel no hesitation in offering help, and in case you feel that it will cause serious problems to you, be sensible enough to refuse by saying a firm and clear 'No'. It is always better to deny at the appropriate hour than to curse yourself later when you suffer for reasons you could have easily avoided. So, please do justice to yourself and learn the art of saying 'No'.

> *It is always better to deny at the appropriate hour than to curse yourself later.*

❑❑❑

19

You Are Your Own Friend

There must have been moments in your life when you got irritated or very annoyed with yourself for some known or unexplained reason. During this time did you ever, or for once, realise who first came to your rescue? If you have observed, or shall now observe, you'll find that it is you yourself. A saying goes that there can be no better friend of you than your ownself and, at the same time, there can be no worst enemy of your's than you yourself. If it is so, then why not prefer to be your own friend. Just try it, I am sure that you will gain a lot of satisfaction for yourself. The problems start budding when we develop the tendency to

> *The problems start budding when we develop the tendency to compete with ourselves.*

compete with ourselves. This fight results in over expectations from our ownself and when these are not met, we feel depressed. One must know that he cannot be a Jack of all trades. If he is an expert in one field, he may be imperfect or ignorant in the other. So, always remember, if you have the ability and can achieve something at one time, you must also be prepared not to let yourself feel disappointed if you loose at the other.

The whole system is like a machine controlled by devine power where every small nut, bolt and other parts have their own importance in proper functioning. Therefore, feel your importance in the system and develop the confidence in yourself. In a football match you cannot expect every member of the winning team to have scored a goal. Surely, there must be someone to play behind and defend; so a defender too has every reason to congratulate himself because though he could not score any goal, he had judiciously served his role as a defender of the net against the other team to make his team win. When you have duties, you have the right to enjoy some privileges too and the foremost right is to take care of your own comfort levels first. Here, it should not be mistaken with selfishness, but the sole idea is that you cannot put others at ease unless you yourself are in a comfortable position. So, you must develop the habit of praising and appreciating yourself even for minor successes because it will help in revitalizing you for facing bigger challenges of life.

There can be no better friend of you than your ownself

It is 'you' only who has and will always accompany you throughout your life. It is you who will bear the burden of your sorrows and so, why don't be your own friend first. If you have you bear your sorrows, then you must also allow yourself to enjoy the pleasure and happiness. Do not feel regretful or disheartened if you fail to attain something according to your wishes; just praise your efforts and promise yourself to do better next time. Feel no harm or guilt in following your own agenda because you are the sole owner of your life and you cannot afford to defer your happiness and contentment for next incarnation, if at all it so happens. You have all the rights to try to fulfil your dreams through genuine efforts, but if sometimes the luck is not bestowed upon you, never bother. A sensible person would always prefer a sustained release of luck rather than one-time blast depriving him of this deciding factor through the rest of his life. So, simply perform your affordable duties and do not hesitate to enjoy your share of the joys of your achievements, because afterall 'you' are your best friend.

It is 'you' only who has and will always accompany you throughout your life. It is you who will bear the burden of your sorrows so, why don't be your own friend first.

❑❑❑

20

Be Happy

The search for happiness is a million-dollar assignment today. Many religious celebrities preach various ways to attain happiness. Their high-profile vocabulary and unrealistic measures put unnecessary load on the mind of the listeners. The biggest truth is that the seedlings of happiness are already embeded within one's core, you only have to nourish them well with optimistic ideas, and the result will be fully grown saplings of joy and satisfaction. Invariably, happiness is the child of satisfaction. You cannot be happy unless you are satisfied and you cannot commit

The biggest truth is that the seedlings of happiness are already embeded within one's core, you only have to nourish it well with optimistic ideas.

that you are satisfied if you are not happy. So, you should have such kind of self-agenda which yields satisfaction as per your requirement. As a sensible human, it is your sole right to keep yourself happy. So, do not hesitate in doing whatever makes you happy. Here, you should also keep in mind that while seeking joy for yourself, you are not plunging others into trouble. You can prove your humanitarianism if, while satisfying yourself you are serving joy to others too, and thus create a situation of real happiness.

Satisfaction means completion or achievement of anything intended. One is free to reach one's desired level of satisfaction through various ways. A particular person may derive satisfaction in making money while some other may do so by achieving the goals, but beware; the happiness may still elude them if there is no set limit for money and if the set goals are unrealistic. They may not achieve desired results because they either do not have the abilities needed for the task or they are simply waiting for miracles to happen. No doubt, the habit of self-discipline is a pre-requisite for achieving goals but your self-discipline should not be so strict that it deprives you of experiencing the joys of your present. It

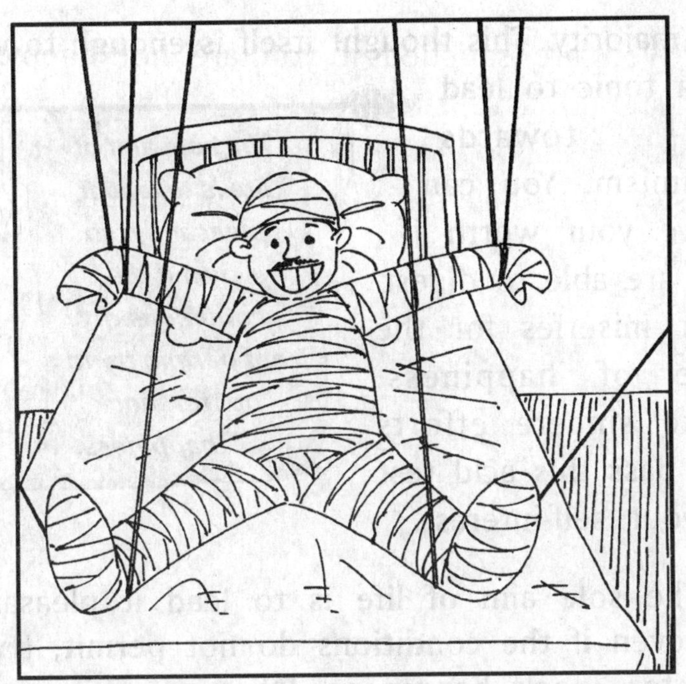

Those who manage to smile, their wounds heal faster

is true that you cannot always ask for happiness, there are bound to be some instances which are unpleasent and sorrowful. The effect of such unfortunate events can be minimized by accepting the fact that we all are puppets in the hands of destiny and the fate, once decided, is inevitable and is bound to smile upon us at the pre-set time.

Just keep in mind that there are fewer people in this world who are happier than you and you are lucky enough to be at a better position than the majority. This thought itself is enough to work as a tonic to lead you towards optimism. You can prove your worth if you are able to digest your miseries for the sake of happiness. Make sincere efforts and pass this acid test in your self-interest.

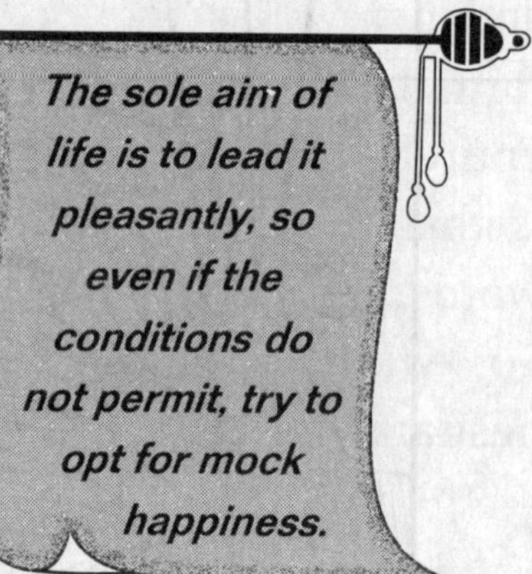

The sole aim of life is to lead it pleasantly. So, even if the conditions do not permit, try to opt for mock happiness. Of course, it cannot replace the real feel of happiness, but at least it will have some soothing effect on you. The culmination of belief within self that one can overcome sad moments is said to have done wonders to many of those suffering from various ailments. It has also been proved that patients who are able to smile through their illness or mishaps, their wounds are likely to heal faster than those who continue to wail. If luckily, you accumulate enough stock of success and happiness, please first retain your portion of it and then distribute the rest among others for the ultimate welfare of society.

Share happy and fun-filled moments with near and dear ones but do not give away your secret formulas responsible for your success. They are entirely your's to conserve. The real magic of life is that the more happiness you distribute by your words and deeds, the more your stocks will grow. So, while trying to make others happy don't hesitate to seek happiness for your own self first.

21

The Truth Of Life

You may be sad today because you could not negotiate one of your problems successfully, but if the reverse had happened, it would have made you very happy. Why should our feelings fluctuate so much and why can't we adopt a uniform reaction towards pros and cons of life? Let it be known that there can be no fixed time bound as to when one's miseries would start or end. Similarly, there is no time limit or time frame for favourable conditions. These two always move parallel to each other in our life. Therefore, it is practically difficult for us to preach anyone to always remain cheerful. But as a sensible human we must ensure that sorrowful memories are short-lived and

Realise the fact that life is full of challenges, and there is no end of them till you leave the world.

occupy very little space in our memory bin. This kind of practice, if adopted, would allow larger room for pleasentries to be stored in our mind and create within us an optimistic, joyful and satisfied individual. Such behavioural change would keep us in pleasent mood and help in shedding off the load of avoidable stresses.

Please realise the fact that life is full of challenges, and there is no end of them till you leave the world. One just cannot elude the ups and downs because they are an integral part of life. It is, therefore, wise to face them boldly and courageously. Under the practical conditions, it is impossible to be a perfectionist. All things do not always happen as per your wish, so be ready to make compromises and adjust-ments according to the demand of situation.

You cannot always keep on fighting against the odds, there must always be space for relaxations. The policy of forget and forgive will certainly help you in maintaing your cool. As the basic truth of life is that you only

You should be wise enough in utilizing every moment of your life.

live once and when you are dead, everything ends for you, so you should be wise enough in utilizing every moment of your life. Develop the habit of sharing your joys and containing your sorrows; do not always weigh the gains and losses; keep yourself ready to face heaven and hell with same attitude and patience.

The theory of satisfaction, which approves that all that has happend was good and will be good, should work as a moral booster to lead us on the path of self-satisfaction. Please learn to forgive yourself first and then only you can have an open attitude towards others. Keep yourself free from unnecessary speculations and evaluations because people who know less think less and are naturally able to enjoy more than those who are over-nursing and susceptive. Never forget that every second gone is nearing you towards your final exit; so, know your limitations and have patience so that you can avoid hurdles in your own path of joy. Here, I may sound a little pessimistic, but the fact is fact: the doomsday is inevitable and nothing is permanent. Then why to complain and whom to complain, just have the positive attitude and sail pleasantly through the odd and even streams of life.

❑❑❑

22

Rights And Responsibilities

It is true that as a superior race we are concerned more about our rights than duties. This tendency creates a situation where everyone is asking for their rights but they are least bothered about their responsibilities. This ultimately proves harmful for the welfare of society and the nation. In ancient times man did not have this problem, but as the races advanced and developed into modern men, the balance tilted towards rights.

The rights and responsibilities need to move parallel to each other. As the head of the family one has the right to rule but at the same time it is his duty to create an environment conducive to the welfare of his whole family. Similarly, as an authentic citizen you have the right to drive on public roads but simultaneously you are responsible to follow the traffic rules to avoid causing problems to others. Clearly, one must give equal weightage to rights and responsibilities.

As per my view, the demand for rights increases with the increase in literacy level of the people. There are chances that an average man can maintain perfect balance between rights and responsi-bilities but a person with high level of intellect would certainly be more demanding for rights than duties. As you go on democratising a system, the people, more and more, demand for rights. Now-a-days, the over-populated democratic countries have started facing this problem; people use rights as tools to take law and order in their own hands. Under such conditions the citizens must be sensitive toward their responsibilities too. Some systems of governance like monarchy and communism, tend to deny even basic fundamental rights to their citizens. Certainly, such condition is also not acceptable because people feel angry and they go on revolt. So far we have failed to develop such a

The demand for rights increases with the increase in literacy level of the people.

political system which gives rights to people with a rider of duties and responsibilities.

If excessive awareness of rights is unjustified, then over-commitment towards duties is also a curse because duties have a unique trend; the more you accept them, the more they will fall on you. No doubt, that complete awareness of rights and the skill with which you exercise them will take you closer to achieving your goals wheareas, if you only engage yourself in fulfilling your duties without knowing and caring for your rights you may become a beast of burden. In the current living trend over-responsible and overtly sincere people are considered laggard because they seldom get an opportunity to taste the fruit of their success. In such self-pathetic situation, the person can only be contended with ornamental praises and verbal appreciations which may serve as a psychological satisfaction. But the end result is that such an overcaring and sacrificing person is often taken 'for granted' by others and he rarely gets

> ***Duties have a unique trend; the more you accept them, the more they will fall on you.***

time to be on his own and look after his self-requirements for success and happiness. Though he may secure social recognition, but ultimately his habit becomes a curse for him.

Give equal weightage to rights and duties

Since excess dose of everything is not recommendable, the excessive sense of duty also needs to be avoided. There has to be a correct balancing of rights and duties so that one can satisfy oneself and at the same time fulfil one's responsibilities, and social obligations also. Always remember that it is your foremost right to make your life comfortable and worth living peacefully. Also, at the same time it is your duty to act in a responsible and sensible manner towards your family, friends and relatives which is ultimately beneficial for society at large.

There has to be a correct balancing of rights and duties.

□□□

23

To Rule Or To Be Ruled

As a normal tendency, no one likes to be ruled, but everyone likes to rule. This conflict between the rulers and those ruled is generating various social disorders. As a human, everyone has the sole right to rule over himself according to his own wishes and convenience, but the real problem arises when others try to dictate him according to their own concepts. Since each individual has his own ideology, one should not expect his near and dear ones to heed only to his rulings.

No one likes to be ruled, but everyone likes to rule.

A child, who aspires to be an engineer, may never become a good doctor even if his or her parents demand so. On the other hand, if the parents provide the child ample information and support, he or she may one day finally become an expert in the chosen field. It is, therefore, wise not to force your likings on others, and if you continue to do so, you are inviting problems for yourself, maybe even malice. Do not force yourself on others. It is always better if one minds his own business. One must realise that as he has been blessed with a life, the others too have only one precious life to live. Therefore, if asked and needed, only then you should 'advise' others but do not feel humiliated if your advices are not heeded.

Do not force yourself on others

Whenever there is a conflict, you must always try to find a mutually amicable solution. Read this real life situation: A healthy Mrs. 'X' is pregnant and the doctors have stated her condition as satisfactory. She wants to continue with her job of an interior designer against the wishes of her husband who 'fears' termination of pregnancy if Mrs. 'X' continues to take the strain of work at home as well as office. Before their arguments turn into a grave problem, they were sensible enough to reach a solution that Mr. 'X', who dislikes cleaning and cooking chores, will help his wife at home till the baby is born and thereafter she can continue her job only after the child begins to go to school. Here no one has ruled anyone and at the same time they have found a satisfactory solution without being forced to change themselves completely.

I am sure that if everyone adopts such kind of cool compromising attitude, the problem of ego clashes and dissatisfaction would minimise automatically. But all our efforts fail when our hyperactive grey matter bypasses all remedial signals and catalyses opposite ideas in our mind. It may sound pleasant that at some instances you have successfully imposed your rulings on others but if your habit of dictating continues, be sure that at some juncture of time they may strongly revolt against you and sever all ties with you.

It is therefore advisable neither to rule and not to be ruled, just adopt the medial path of life. Follow the motto "live and let live". Before floating any advice, try to become a patient listener, lubricate your shock absorbers within you, evaluate patiently and reveal limited reactions to a particular situation. If you are kind enough to honour the sentiments of others, then only expect others to be sensitive towards your emotions.

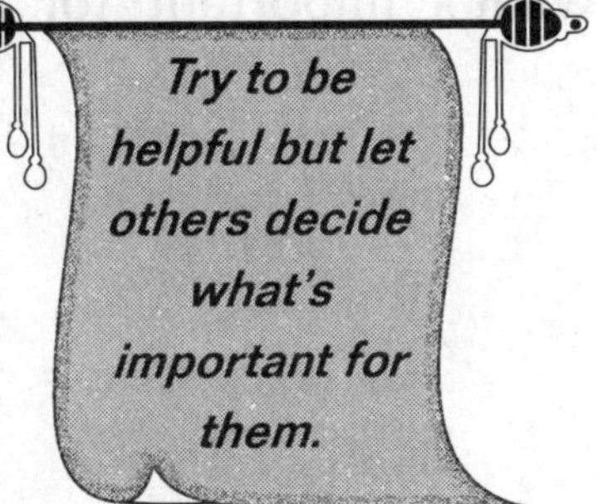

As a general practice it is very easy to give directions and preach ideology to others but it is very difficult to follow it yourself. As a friend, philosopher and guide, you should only advise and give suggestions to your near and dear ones, but do not expect or force them to follow you in totality. They have their own decision-making levels and will decide what to do depending on their requirements. Try to imagine yourself in their situation. Would you accept anything from others that does not seem appropriate to you to follow blindly? Your answer will be 'No'. So, in order to maintain healthy and balanced relationships, please refrain from the habit of ruling and dictating others. Try to be helpful but let others decide what's important for them.

24

Judge Yourself

Your birth as human race is the mightiest gift of destiny. Had Almighty not been kind enough, he would have made you some other living creature, may be an insect or an animal. Your advanced 'thinking' brain and limbs are a boon to you, so why don't you use them. There seems to be no reason why you should underestimate yourself; know your potential and don't hesitate in your optimizing abilities. Do not let yourself be branded as 'looser'. Keep the window of transactions open, be broadminded and view yourself positively in this world because life is precious enough and not be wasted. It must be realised that underestimating yourself is equally

Underestimating yourself is equally harmful as overestimation. In both cases we fail to assess our efficiencies.

harmful as overestimation. In both cases we fail to assess our efficiencies.

Don't give up just like that. Try man! You can also win

Opportunities do not always come uniformly, sometimes they arrive automatically and sometimes you have to hunt for them. The former ones are gift of the Almighty and must be exploited on top priority; the latter opportunities open up after your efforts only. Don't be afraid to avail of opportunities that come your way. Don't waste time arguing with yourself whether you are capable or not to use the opportunity successfully. Each one of us is capable of doing a task successfully in some way or the other. So, don't just sit back and miss the chance. Underestimating yourself will only take away your peace of mind. Whereas, if you are confident of your moves you may very well succeed. We must admit that results are beyond our control and one can only put on his best efforts. So, don't be a miser in putting forward your best efficiencies. It will generate two possibilities: if you succeed, be proud of not underestimating yourself and thank the Almighty. But if you do not get the desired result, still praise your efforts and promise yourself that next time you will try to do better.

We must admit that results are beyond our control and one can only put on his best efforts. So, don't be a miser in putting forward your best efficiencies.

Sometimes we waste away even the good chances that come our way simply due to fear of failure which ultimately creates depression. Life offers you your part of fortune at an appropriate time and in pre-decided quantum, but this thought should not make you feel low and stop you from search of better options for your satisfaction. This is the time when your confidence levels must be put forward. They tend to boost your morale and do not let you waste any opportunity. But beware, don't overestimate youself. Overconfidence will not get you anywhere. Chances are that the failure not being able to do something successfully — will add to your depression. The end result would be that you will underestimate yourself further. So, take care to have and maintain a balanced approach.

You have no reason to curse yourself because it is a normal human habit to make mistakes; and failures too are the part of life. We can make ourselves stronger if we continue to learn from our mistakes and losses. Very often, we tend to underestimate ourselves when we think from the heart instead of the mind. The extra room for emotions lead us away from right thinking and planning. When you underestimate yourself you tend to keep yourself away from many activities and gradually loose confidence. You become aloof and people begin to ignore you. Don't let this happen. Have the confidence within you, make good assessment of your positive abilities, set your priorities and choose the most suitable opportunity. Your efforts are bound to bring out positive results.

❑❑❑

25

Forgive And Forget

The idea of forgive and forget stands on the foundation of basic theory of live and let live. If followed judiciously, this theory is sure to provide the much needed relief from our anger and miseries. Why should we be bothered about unfavourable happenings around us? Be assurred that final settlements are not under our control, the destiny will settle all scores automatically before one makes a final exit. Let it be well known that you are your own baby, therefore the entire liability of proper nursing rests on your own shoulders. You may have to face criticism for the actions you deemed fit. Just hear

If followed judiciously, the theory of forgive and forget provides the much needed relief from anger and miseries.

it patiently, accept it if you think it is beneficial, otherwise reject it without revealing any reaction. The Newton's theory that every action has a reaction, does not apply exactly on the human behaviour. A peaceful person may not react to every action taken towards him but if his reacting is a must he may first judge the outcome, or may even defer it for some other appropriate time if the present tidings are not in his favour.

Our capacity to retain memories is the greatest hurdle in following the concept of forget and forgive. Every human brain has retaining power, but it has the tendency to retain sorrowful memories for a longer period than the happier and pleasant one's. To remain at peace, this pattern must be reversed; the unpleasant memories must be locked away and happier one's be shared again and again so that they stay in the mind's forefront. But, we tend to

Our inner feeling of goodness and inbuilt sense of ethics will definitely promote the act of forgetting the sad parts in our life thus letting us forgive those who caused us pain.

remember the hurt and pain others have caused us promising ourselves never to forget them. We need to be optimistic that people are basically good and some drawback of their's must have been the reason for unintentionally hurting us. Our inner feeling of goodness and inbuilt sense of ethics will definitely promote the act of forgetting the sad parts in our life thus letting us forgive those who caused us pain.

"It's OK! you made a mistake but be careful not to play near any glass window again."

Please realise that as you have been gifted with only one life span and you want to live it your own way, the others too have a single life time and they also have the right to avail of it as per their wish. This does not mean others have the right to hurt you. No doubt, certain people can harm you physically or mentally but if the act has been done involuntarily then it is a case of forgiveness, and if it has been done with intention, then don't revenge but take defensive measures so that the same event does not get repeated. By doing so, you have not proved yourself to be weak; instead you have sensibly conveyed that you are a genuine human. Through the habit of pardoning you relieve yourself from anxiety and unnecessary tensions. On the other hand, the person forgiven has a feeling of shame and guilt for himself which prevents him from repeating the action in future. Remember, one who forgives is superior to the one who is forgiven.

While deciding to forgive and forget, one should not be over calculative and should not speculate things which, under severe conditions, may result in some form of psychological disorder. All acts cannot be assessed in terms of profit and gains; so don't waste time in thinking how to forgive. It cannot be denied that we easily forgive ourself when we hurt someone and forget the incident, so in the same way forgive others and move on. By forgiving someone you may have to surrender your ego, but at the same time you gain appreciation on humanitarian grounds. This will give more peace to your mind then keeping the thought of revenge or having grudges against the other person.

Therefore, do remember that everyone, including yourself, has shortcomings which are quite naturally a part of life. So, be generous in forgiving not just yourself but others also and forget such instances for a happier tomorrow.

26

The Feeling Of Guilt

Are you feeling bad because you could not achieve what you intended, or unknowingly you have hurt someone? Please try to contain yourself and don't feel any guilt. Accept the fact that you cannot set all things right always and some mishappenings are bound to occur. Don't feel inadequate about yourself. If others can digest their guilt, why can't you? Let your self-confidence dominate over guilt.

The feeling of being guilty for anything that went wrong gives birth to pessimistic feelings inside you, which ultimately may diminish your efficiency. If this feeling lingers for longer time, you tend to undergo depression which reduces chances of positivity in thoughts. Under these circumstances people take advantage of your guilt and try to exploit your personality for their own benefits. So, please do learn to control your emotions for your own good, think from your mind and not from your heart. Analyse whatever happened and you may find that there is no reason for being guilty.

Thinking the other way, the feeling of guilt is not that bad because it helps to keep our behaviour within social norms. It is a psychological feeling which compells us to take the appropriate actions in order to compensate our past mistakes. It is true that being a civilized creature you cannot escape feeling guilty for mistakes but surely you can minimise its effect by promising yourself that it will not be repeated in future. You cannot allow your guilt to steal your peace of mind, therefore pardon yourself for your own satisfaction. The wiser people instead of being guilty for something take it as a challenge and try to mould things for their benefit in future. If too much guilt is harmful, total lack of it is also not right as it can lead to the making of a defective personality. In

> ***Guilt is a psychological feeling which compells us to take the appropriate actions in order to compensate our past mistakes.***

the absence of any guilt, if one keeps on repeating the same mistakes, he falls in the category of shameless persons who have no respect for civilized values.

It is normal, feel no guilt. Buy a new pot.

If Mr. 'X' is feeling guilty because he accidently damaged the car he borrowed from his friend, his guilt is justified but he must take remedial action soon and get the car fully repaired before returning it. Had he returned it in the same damaged condition, he would have entered the category of careless selfish persons. If the damage to the car is not visible but is in the knowledge of Mr. X and he still returns the car neither without getting it repaired nor intimating his friend about it along with an honest apology, it is not an appreciable act. What if Mr. X's friend meets with a fatal accident? Will Mr. X ever be able to get rid of the guilt of not doing the right thing at the required time and losing his friend due to his own act of negligence or foolishness? Surely, the answer is 'never'. Feeling guilty of something going wrong is a normal behaviour but it should not have a prolonged effect on one's psychology. Let the feeling be short lived and fulfil the promise of not repeating the mistakes in future. Apart from this please don't forget to take precautionary measures to reduce the impact of damages done innocently or voluntarily.

If you want to avoid the situations where you have to fight the feeling of guilt, try to be careful in whatever you do and take care that nothing bad or wrong happens knowingly; and be prepared to accept your mistakes and apologize even if you have unintentionally been the cause of hurt or loss to others.

❑❑❑

27

You Never Miss A Bus

When people fail to achieve the desired goal, it is termed as "missing the bus". But I assure you, it is never late than ever; you never miss a bus because there are thousands of buses still to come in the form of opportunities, which you can take to reach your destination. So, if you don't succeed in a particular section, please don't feel lost or insecure. Be sure that at some juncture you are bound to get your share of luck. The life, particularly the human behaviour, is such a vast and variant subject that you cannot lay down rules of governance applicable uniformly to all.

As I have already stated that life is too precious to involve yourself in measuring successes and failures, always be assured that nobody can rob you of your fortunes fixed by the destiny. Let it be known that if there are problems then there are solutions too; you cannot force solutions as per your own will; many matters automatically get settled in the conducive environment. It also depends on how able and quick you are in grabbing the opportunity.

A particular student may develop the phobia for competitive exams because he could not earlier qualify a few of them thus preventing him further from making his natural efforts. But this must not be the end of his career or his future prospects. Here, he must realise that failure in a few exams does not close the gates of getting success in all exams. What he needs to do is to appear at those exams which match his mental calibre. Since you are the best judge of your life, don't be biased in assessing yourself judiciously and then select your goals as per your calibre. It is only you who knows it better what you can do and what you cannot. Therefore, choose what you can achieve easily with your sincere efforts and thus you can

There is always room for errors in life, so committing a few of them does not deprive you of further opportunities.

prevent yourself from all kinds of avoidable stresses.

Please do not panic, take the next bus

Our problems start when we opt for unrealistic goals, and thus invite the risk of failures. Many people may laugh at your attempts yielding negative results but never bother because you at least had the courage to attempt it. The idea that you had put down your genuine efforts should be strong enough to make you feel satisfied of yourself. If you loose some opportunity never feel disheartened; instead plan for your goal properly and wait patiently for some other opportunity. Be convinced that life gives many opportunity. Every individual has to decide for himself which one he must avail. It is like taking the right bus to reach your desired destination. Instead of running after each and every bus be must be sure of where you have to go.

As a sensible person one should give equal weightage to success and failure; the successes breeds feeling of satisfaction while the failures teach us lessons for future. The life keeps on offering us the chances and we are free to avail of them or refuse them. You can take full liberty in choosing the chances of your choice but at the same time don't always expect the positive results. There is always room for errors in life, so committing a few of them does not deprive you of further opportunities. You have the right to plan for your goals and be happy and contented. Just feel happy about your efforts and be optimistic that some better opportunity is in the waiting for you. Therefore, keep in mind that any number of opportunities or chances lost is not the end of the world for you.

❑❑❑

28

Gain Without Pain

The preachings of "first learn to bear pain and then think of gains" are now history because they promote the idea of sacrificing your present for the hope of a good future. Having gone through this book so far, the readers must have realised that I am against the above mentioned theory. I prefer that you should go only for limited gains for which you need not bear any pain. The pain in any form is deplorable and must be avoided because it is the ugliest thing which needs to be eluded. Though today we have doctors and medicines to cure our physical pains, the remedy for mental or psychological agonies are still lacking. But

The pain in any form is deplorable and must be avoided because it is the ugliest things which needs to be eluded.

sometimes, the temptation for gains is so intense that we start compromising with our present.

A student, who is very intelligent and laborious, may succeed in securing a lucrative career but it is not necessary that as an adult he will be satisfied from within. The thought that he had sacrified his childhood & adulthood will always haunt him. Many parents are known to send their children to boarding schools because they think that by doing so they are gaining time for their senseless socializing, and the boarding teachers can take care of their child's future. But, the agony of their life is that they miss the sweet company of their child and his naughty activities thus leaving no childish memories at all. This is being done only for the child's bright future, which is uncertain.

Now let us think: Is it really necessary to send the children away and deprive them of parental nursing? Is it right that children go through emotional pain and parents gain on their social circle? The answer will always be negative in this case. Parents should make it a rule that they denote ample time to their children for their good upbringing and also plan their socializing, involving their children also on some occasions.

At no cost should anyone sacrifice a pleasurable present for future. What we gain today will definitely stay but if we do not gather it today, we may be at total loss tomorrow if there is nothing for us on that day.

It is good to receive gains for your past actions, but you can never be sure that when and how much will they be because, as we know, the destiny will play its role. I know that hard efforts are necessary in life but they should only be exerted upto the magnitude till they do not cause you stress. Just be patient, make efforts as per your ability and priority and forget about the results. A soldier causing maximum damage to the enemy without hurting himself is always to be preferred to the soldier who unfortunately gets hurt at the border without facing the enemy. So, always welcome the gains attained with justified quantum of pains.

Hard efforts are necessary in life but they should only be exerted upto the magnitude till they do not cause you stress.

❑❑❑

29

Race Against Time

Are you racing against time? Please beware of this habit because it is something beyond human capabilities. Time runs faster than our thoughts, making every second of life very precious. The passage of time is irreversible, the time once gone is gone for ever; we just cannot bring it back. It is therefore, one's prime duty to honour its value. The time is adamant, we cannot mould it according to our wishes because it is governed by destiny. It is always preferable to adopt the policy of wait and watch so that we can make use of our efforts according to the need of time. Here, if we try to act faster, the time will defeat us. Therefore, always let time remain ahead of us. People often say that life is short but according to me, it is adequate. Yes, we make it shorter when we try to run against time *i.e.,* either we do too little or try to do much more than what the time permits us to do.

The time is very eventful; it has many surprises for us which are released sustainably at different points of time. Some of these events are pleasent and some are sorrowful. We cannot be selective in accepting them, both are to be taken as they are. We cannot dictate time to give us favourable results. We can only put down our best efforts and be positive in hoping that the Almighty will give us our share of luck. We also don't know the nature of time, its pendulum keeps on swinging to the either sides. When it is favourable, even our minimum efforts are enough in bringing success but when it is not, our very genuine efforts also fail. There is no doubt that however prosperous and influential you are, you cannot tame time to do you favour.

> *There is no doubt that however prosperous and influential you are, you cannot tame time to do you favour.*

It has been rightly said that you cannot expect anything before due time just as you cannot expect more than that decided by destiny. I stress again that one should, therefore, not develop anxiety because one is bound to receive his share of luck at an appropriate time and in pre-decided quantity. The time is also naughty in nature; it always escapes our hold and moves on its own way. It does not demarcate wins and losses or successes and failures because they all are an integral part of its composition.

You can not run faster than time

I always believe that the lesser we know, the lesser are the stresses. Therefore. let us thank God that we don't exactly know our future, we can only speculate on the basis of our efforts. We continue to live, think and work because we don't know what the time will serve us in future. If we know all what future has in store for us, it would become hard to live mainly because of the approaching bad times. The value of time will diminish and there will be no charm for the future. This could be the reason that time has its own pace. So, when you cannot change or dominate time, you should surrender and go with it. Accept everything that it brings, think optimistically and continue to hope for the favourable time to greet you.

30

The Key For Solutions

Born as humans with improved grey matter, we are sensitive enough to feel the impact of problems. Till the time we are living, we continue to face diversified problems. Since we cannot escape every problem, the hunt for the solutions continues forever. Let it be well-known that patience is the pre-requisite for all solutions. It is mandatory that every solution should be able to satisfy the current needs, and it must show the precautionary steps for the future. If an insect bites on our leg we immediately shake the leg to throw it away; this kind of action is a reflex solution which does not need any use of intellect. Some problems are common in nature which everyone has to face on regular basis, so their solutions are also simple and defined. If you fall sick, go to a doctor; if your

> ***Patience is the pre-requisite for all solutions.***

automobile or any domestic appliance is out of order you call the mechanic; and if your child is weak in a particular subject you send him for the specific subject tutorials. The above problems are very common, so instead of taking undue stress you simply use your sources to get the solution.

If you match the right key, the lock will certainly open

Another type of problems are specific in nature: they either fall on us as misfortunes or they may be the result of our misjudgements or mistakes. First of all, as a sensitive creature, we should take all prior remedial steps so that such situations do not arise. And if they do arise then we must have enough courage to combat them. Mr. X is worried because his son is very susceptible to measles which affects his studies. Had he got his child vaccinated in due course, this problem could have been avoided. The basic theory that no problem exists without remedy, should encourage you to face it boldly. If a complex problem arises, be patient, evaluate it, recollect your own past experiences or any such experiences told to you by someone else, search for the possible solutions and then choose the final remedy suiting your abilities and resources to tackle and control the disturbing situation. We all know that if we match the right key, the lock will certainly open. Similary, the right solutions will always remove the problems that we face in our life's journey.

The basic theory that no problem exists without remedy should encourage you to face it boldly.

It is also a possibility that even after your best efforts you may fail to find the remedy for some problem. In such case, it is not your fault; so first seek help. If nothing works, then put such problems aside, they may get solved naturally with the passage of time and if it still remains, learn to bear and live with it. Here, you can convince yourself by the simple thought that you are not the Almighty; so all the solutions are not within your reach. Be sure that at some juncture the destiny will come to your rescue and you are bound to get the reward for your efforts and patience. Therefore, have no sorrows, no agony and no complaints or regrets, and keep yourself prepared to boldly accept whatever your life has offered to you.

31

Prove Your Worth

You are precious not only for yourself but also for your family, friends and relations, and for the nation too. Therefore, kindly know your worth to generate positive values within yourself and leave no room for negative emotions. Think more from your mind than your heart, because you know that even your minor action can have a long lasting impact on your own life as well as on the life of others, shows your logical strength. Do not forget that we are equally potent physically: we have a developed mind to think well, tongue to speak well and enabled limbs to perform well, so just maintaining proper and appropriate coordination between them proves your physical, emotional and social abilities. It is man who has built megastructures, the dams, harnessed atomic

A man's worth is known by what he does and how?

power, and explored the space, but at the same time he has also created atom bomb, lethal weapons and terrorism. A man's worth is known by what he does, and how.

You are priceless

Know the fact that you have to shoulder many responsibilities; your family needs your support, your near and dear ones need your company, and your nation needs your contribution. You cannot elude your duties; you can defer them for a while but it is ultimately you who has to do them.

In order to earn respect, regard, honour and recognition, you have to prove your worth. It is not difficult to prove your worth in the field which matches your liking and ability. Here, you can't afford to hesitate or waste time. If you have your priorities set in their due order and are honestly attending to them, you have proved yourself to a great extent. Your achieved success, without neglecting your duties and responsibilities, is the best marker of your worth. Now, you are priceless in the eyes of all around you. Beyond this, there is nothing more you can ask the Almighty to give you for making you happy and contended with life.

32

Have You Played Your Role?

While negotiating various conditions in life, we seldom spare time to assess our own role, instead we keep on asking questions to others. It is, therefore, of utmost importance that we must have some free time in between to judge our own performance at different stages. As a self-guided person you should always follow the system of self-questioning and must regularly make your own queries. You need not invite anyone else to be a judge because you yourself are your best judge. The judgement should be based on a single parameter *i.e.,* your own level of satisfaction. Here, do not estimate your successes and wins, just count your efforts and if you think they were adequate then you

As a self guided person you should always follow the system of self-questioning.

have every reason to feel satisfied because you have played your role to the best of your abilities. If you feel that you have lacked at some juncture, feel no regrets because one can never be perfect always — the humanitarian limitations and weaknesses play their own part.

Do justice with the roles to the best of your ability

You are a good child if you grow upto the expectations of your parents. However, once you are settled, have a job and get married, then your own role starts. Now first of all you have to prove yourself as a good husband or wife. After you have children, you need to prove yourself as a good parent. You have to nurse and educate your children as per your resources and concentrate on your career for the sake of satisfactory living. Please don't forget that you have obligations and duties towards your ageing parents also. They may not demand financial support but they certainly need due respect and care. In modern living the urge for success and win is so strong that many of us unintentionally happen to overlook all our social responsibilities. This problem usually increases where both husband and wife are working and their soaring ambition for successful career leads to selfish attitude where mostly the children grow in neglect. In the race to win, the mutual respect and family cohesion breaks resulting in a non-sensitive society. It is, therefore, important to know our actual needs so that we can apply only pre-decided quantum of efforts to get the desired

Life is really pleasent, so be very simple and sensible in performing your role.

satisfaction, both at professional and at domestic platform.

You must remember that there is no limit of desires, so try to contain them and match with your resources and abilities. When the gap between aspirations and abilities widens, it brings frustration and encourages pessimism. I, surely don't ask for an escapist attitude, instead you must play your role according to the demand of situation. Be sensible enough not to choose difficult roles, which mismatch your aptitude and pose a threat to your personality. The life is really very pleasant, so be very simple and sensible in performing your role; don't be over enthusiastic, utilize your opportunities, perform to the best of your efforts and patiently wait for results. Be flexible and make compromises in situations which put you and others at ease. Also, do not aspire for gains which are beyond your reach; just feel satisfied that your share of destiny can be delayed but it can never elude you. Play your role efficiently by being honest to your true-self.

❑❑❑

33

Now Be Slow And Retard

No doubt, many of you have led an active and satisfactory life, but certainly this phase cannot continue forever because after a particular age your abilities start to retard. There is no harm in accepting that your plane has already landed and now you can afford to loosen your seat belts. Normally, this period arrives when you are on the verge of completing your sixtees. Your social obligations must have been met, and all your duties well performed, so now it is the right time to shed off your responsibilities by passing them on the other active members of your family.

At this juncture of life try to seek pleasure from the sweet memories of the past and avoid the bitter ones. Stop worrying about some work you may not have been able to complete and seek satisfaction that throughout your life you have performed to the best of your abilities and you are not responsible for any losses in situations that were beyond your control.

The psychology of life is so vast and complicated that you cannot keep on fighting at all fronts, so leave some matters to under-go autodegeneration and some problems for auto-solution. As the flowing water finds its own path, leave all your worries in the strong hands of destiny, be a passive thinker and learn to relax, to enjoy the rest of your life. It is a well-known human weakness that everyone tends to escape the ultimate truth called death. When we know it is inevitable, why can't we proceed towards it in a graceful manner? Instead, it is observed that the more and more we inch towards our end, the more affinity we generate towards life; this ultimately increases the fear of death.

When we know death is inevitable, why can't we proceed towards it in a graceful manner?

According to Hindu mythology, the head of a family after reaching a certain age, used to migrate for vanaprastha, which meant self-exile to forests in search of peace and getting mentally prepared for a final decent exit from the world. But currently this theory is of academic importance only and cannot be followed. However, we can infer that it meant: the time of withdrawal from all kinds of profits and losses that may disturb your peace. I never advocate that a long life span should not be welcomed but one must be cautious that this delayed departure does not cause any kind of inconvenience to others and yourself too.

Come to an easy stop at your destination

So, realise that now it is the right time to slow down, because after sixtees you don't have much left to gain or loose. Therefore, by this time, have no new plans, no regrets and no complaints; just accept the things, feel completely satisfied within yourself and do whatever pleases you. Finally, pray to the Almighty to secure a cozy berth for you in heaven.

34

Praise Yourself

Life is meant for living, and living happily. It is not necessary that you burden yourself for becoming successful. If you are happy, you are definitely successful. Also, there is no defined rule that you can make remarkable achievements only when you grow into an adult. At every stage of life, you achieve something of importance. Good results, high educational and professional qualifications, selection for a satisfying job, a happy family life, a tension free old age, and so on, are all achievements at different levels. Helping others and developing a positive attitude can't be left behind. Such acts are achievements of your personality.

I am sure that you must have achieved something creditable in your life. You do not have to be a big shot industrialist or a celebrity to win praise; you only need the recognition of being a sensible, stable and helpful person. If you are aware of your responsibilities and performing your duties efficiently, you need not worry about what everyone says or comments. If people around you, your near and dear ones, are happy that you are doing your best, you certainly deserve a pat on your back. If you are not excessively success crazy, you are leading a simple yet contended life. You know what is required of, or expected from, you and what exactly you have to do. You have a balanced approach towards your workings, and the results which you get satisfy you.

You have every right to congratulate yourself for each achievement of your's.